A LANDSCAPE OF LETTERS

~ with haiku

Written and illustrated by Fiona Sinclair

Walk in the landscape
listen to the pulse of life—
pick up your pen. Write!

Published by:

38/1631 Wynnum Road
Tingalpa Qld 4173
Australia.
www.boolarongpress.com.au

First published 2025

A catalogue record for this book is available from the National Library of Australia

ISBN: 9781923321038 (Paperback)

Printed and bound by Watson Ferguson & Company, Tingalpa, Australia

A Landscape of Letters is an illustrated haiku book about the natural world.

These poems are moments of significance to me as I walk and observe the Australian landscape. I look closely at the bending alpine wild flowers and walk quietly in the hope to see the platypus in feathery reeds. I sit by the pond to catch a glimpse of the darting dragonfly and wonder at the dance of the Monarch butterfly as it flits from flower to flower.

The aim of this book is to inspire you to go outside, observe what is around you and write your own haiku.

walk in the landscape
listen to the pulse of life—
pick up your pen. Write!

There are tips and hints for writing haiku at the back of the book.

Aa

alpine daisies bloom
trigger plants fling pollen dose
summer insects fly

Alpine wildflowers

Bb

blown towards the coast
bogong moths' spring migration
billy buttons bend

Billy button and bogong moth

Cc

screeching high above
seed pod hurtles downward—ouch!
clumsy cockatoo?

Cockatoo

Dd

skimming and darting
the dragonfly zigzags past—
jewel in the sky

Dragonfly

Ee

slow, tough echidna
ball of spikes when under threat
a vanishing act

Echidna

Ff

yellow and black stripes
how can this frog of poison
sound like a wet squelch?

Gg

ancient goanna
slowly sways towards the egg—
swallows in one gulp

Goanna

Hh

ghost-like heron. Still—
waiting in the shallows to
strike with long, sharp beak!

Ii

buzzing, chirping sounds
the arrival of summer—
insects on my skin

Jj

brooch on the wattle
jewel beetle glinting bright—
lucky charm or pest?

Jewel beetle

Kk

spring buds reach out to
shake hands—the kangaroo paw's
velvety fingers

Kangaroo paw

Ll

the greatest mimic—
is it a flute or chainsaw?
superb lyrebird's song

Lyrebird

Mm

black and orange dance
in my butterfly garden—
migrating monarchs

Monarch butterfly

Nn

searching for termites
long tongue delves—solitary
endangered numbat

Numbat

Oo

an orange belly
future children will not see
here. Now—in the tree

Orange-bellied parrot

Pp

a winter delight—
broad-billed platypus dive deep
in feathery reeds

Platypus

Qq

quintessential quoll
sharp teeth, furry, pointed snout
spotted—in the wild

Quoll

Rr

birds dipped in bright paint—
rosella nests in tall trees
bell-like sounds drift by

Rosella parrot

Ss

wrapped in mystery
following shimmering scents
of seaweed and shells

Seaweed and shells

Tt

living near the reefs
trumpetfish—like a long straw
suck prey and swallow

Trumpetfish

Uu

named the Ulysses
attractive to predators—
trappings of beauty

Ulysses butterfly

Vv

variegated
fairy-wren—shrill, bold and bright
cotton ball on pins

Variegated fairy-wren

Ww

fiery red head
long leathery razored leaves
wild, free waratah

Waratah

Xx

Xanthotis flits—skips
foraging in the tree fruit
eyes darting here—there

Xanthotis

Yy

detecting the string
yabby burrows underground
superb blue claws dig

Yabby

Zz

moving in currents
drifting tiny animals—
zooplankton give life

Zooplankton

How to write haiku poetry

Traditional Japanese haiku are poems that date back to the 13th century. Haiku often incorporates images from nature and seasonal changes. Over time, poets began exploring other themes and now haiku explores many themes and topics. The simplicity makes it accessible to people of almost any reading level, making this type of poetry ideal for the classroom.

The theme in A Landscape of Letters focuses on the natural world - the flora and fauna in the Australian landscape. The poems look at the bending alpine wildflowers, the platypus in feathery reeds, a glimpse of the darting dragonfly, the dance of the monarch butterfly and others.

To write your own haiku, select a moment that has some significance for you. The sound of the school bell at home time, the smell of your favourite meal, the feeling of a warm jumper, or something as simple as sharpening a pencil, picking a flower or listening to the rain. Haiku can be funny or serious, modern or traditional, about nature or the modern world.

In regard to grammar and punctuation, some poets begin with a lower case letter and do not end with a full stop to allow the haiku to flow and appear open-ended. Colons and dashes are used to create a pause, rather than a comma, and a question mark is used to suggest mystery.

Look at the examples of others to see the style of punctuation that suits your haiku.

What are the rules for structuring a haiku?

- It has three lines.
- It has five syllables in the first and third lines.
- It has seven syllables in the second line.
- Its lines don’t rhyme.
- It may refer to nature and the seasonal changes.
- It can focus on a small moment like a raindrop falling or a feather floating in the air.
- It can be funny.
- It can have a surprise in the last line.

Teaching notes

1. Explain what haiku is – the traditional history and types of haiku that are written today.
2. Explain how to construct haiku using the 5/7/5 rule of five syllables in the first line, seven syllables in the second line and five syllables in the third line.
3. Review children's knowledge of syllables and clap along to the syllables in words.
4. Explore themes. These can be traditional themes of nature and the landscape, modern themes or funny themes. Read some examples to illustrate the different themes.
5. Brainstorm words. Write a list of words that relate to the chosen theme – what it looks like, sounds like, feels like, smells like.
6. Write the first line of five syllables.
7. Write the second line of seven syllables.
8. Write the third line of five syllables.
9. Remember that sometimes haiku have a surprise in the last line.

Theme ideas

- Write a haiku about an animal/ object/person and see if others can guess what it is.
- Look around the room and choose an object to write about. For example, looking out the window, the carpet, an artwork on the wall, a container of coloured pencils.
- Go into the playground at school and sit quietly and write about the sounds that you can hear.
- Choose an animal such as a pet, a favourite animal or an extinct or endangered animal as a theme.

heading home on foot
pages of poems that sing
my haiku journey